Unlocking the Wealth Vault

Secrets to Greed-Proof Happiness

Robert K. Wylie

Table of Contents

Introduction

Money and the Mind - Unmasking the Financial Wizard Within

There was a woman named Emma who lived in the sleepy hamlet of Willowbrook. When it came to creating a budget, conserving money from her income, and making wise investments, Emma had always been diligent. Her meticulous handling of her finances was frequently admired by her acquaintances. "You're like a financial wizard, Emma," people would remark.

Emma got a surprise windfall one terrible day. She had received a big fortune from a distant cousin. She first believed that this unexpected money would offer her boundless joy. But as time went on, Emma began to experience fear and uncertainty. She was immobilized by the worry of losing what she had acquired and resisted making any financial decisions.

The tale of Emma is not unusual. It emphasizes a key truth: psychology has a significant influence on how we

behave financially. Our perspective on money is greatly influenced by our upbringing, experiences, and even emotions. Whether we're conscious of it or not, unseen forces within our thoughts frequently influence how we make financial decisions.

We will go alongside Emma and the numerous other people who have struggled with their own money attitudes across the pages of this book. We'll solve the psychological puzzles underlying our financial decisions together. We'll investigate how feelings like fear, greed, and happiness affect our choices and learn useful techniques for coordinating our financial objectives with our money mentality.

So, if you've ever wondered how to use the power of your mind for financial success, why you occasionally overspend, or why you feel concerned about making financial decisions, you're about to go on an exciting trip. Join us as we reveal the financial genius you possess—the money mindset that controls your future financial well-being.

There was a woman named Emma who lived in the sleepy hamlet of Willowbrook. Emma was well-known for her uncompromising financial caution across the neighborhood. She was good at planning her spending, meticulously conserving a percentage of her income, and making investments that appeared to be wise. You're like a financial magician, Emma, and her friends and relatives would comment on her methodical approach to money.

But Emma was oblivious to the huge effect of her own thoughts on her financial decisions, which lay hidden under this façade of financial freedom. Emma's tendency for frugal living and her cautious approach to investing were strongly ingrained in her background and experiences. She had a strong dread of financial instability because her parents had experienced their fair share of financial troubles. She had unconsciously adopted a money mindset that was motivated by fear and scarcity.

Emma got a surprise windfall one terrible day. She had scarcely known the distant cousin who had given her a significant inheritance. At first, she thought that this unanticipated amount of money would offer her boundless joy and financial comfort. However, Emma saw that her skepticism and concern grew as the days progressed into weeks.

She was gripped by the worry of losing what she had acquired and resisted making any important financial decisions. The possibilities and possible perils of her newfound money kept her up at night, tormented. Emma's formerly careful money management has changed into a constant internal conflict.

Emma's tale highlights a basic fact about the financial industry and is not a unique incident. Our psychological makeup has a significant impact on our financial behavior. Our upbringing, life experiences, and the emotional rollercoaster that frequently follows financial decisions all have an impact on it. Whether we are conscious of it or not, unseen forces within our thoughts regularly influence our financial decisions.

We'll see Emma again as we set out on this voyage into the core of financial psychology and follow her as she experiences the highs and lows of her financial journey. Emma's financial adventure is not, however, an isolated one. Numerous other people have struggled with the mystery of their own money attitudes, and their experiences are shared by many people. We'll solve the psychological puzzles underlying our financial decisions together.

Chapter 1

The Wealth Paradox - Unraveling the Mystery of What Money Can and Can't Buy

Money plays a significant part in our lives because of its universal attraction and unmistakable effect. It serves as the medium of exchange for aspirations and wishes, a method of securing comfort and opportunity, and a potent instrument for negotiating the challenges of contemporary life. On the other hand, when we go through the realm of riches, we come upon a paradox—a careful balance between what money can and cannot purchase.

The Allure of Abundant Money

Let's start with the intriguing aspect of the situation. Money has an unmistakable draw since it is sometimes portrayed as the panacea to all of life's desires. It gives us the means to fulfill our fundamental needs and turn our goals into reality. What money can be purchased in further detail is as follows:

At its most fundamental level, money offers the tools to guarantee our material comfort. It provides us with the necessities, including housing, food, clothes, and medical care. We ensure our fundamental requirements with the financial resources at our disposal, laying the groundwork for a pleasant life.

Experiences: Money has the ability to influence lives in ways that go beyond material goods. It opens the doors to experiences like visiting far-off places, going to events, enjoying fine dining, and taking part in activities that enhance our lives. These encounters let one live a life that is actually enjoyed rather than merely endured.

Chances: Financial resources open doors to chances for personal development, job success, and academic study. Our dreams may be funded by money, enabling us to broaden our horizons and fully realize our potential.

Peace of Mind: Money has an impact on our mental health. Through insurance, emergency savings, and financial stability, it may provide us peace of mind. Anxiety is reduced and a sense of security is fostered when we are aware that we have a safety net in the event of uncertainty.

Freedom: When we are financially independent, we are free to choose according to our tastes rather than our means. It gives us the freedom to follow our passions, partake in fulfilling activities, and live our lives as we see fit.

Money makes it easier to be comfortable and convenient. It enables us to outsource duties, delegate chores, and make use of services that simplify our lives. These conveniences free up our time for the things that really count, from housekeeping to transportation.

The Mysterious Pursuit of Happiness

We come into a dilemma that has puzzled philosophers and intellectuals throughout history—the pursuit of happiness—amid the material advantages that money bestows. Money may undoubtedly improve our quality of life, but it cannot provide pleasure in and of itself. This paradox draws attention to the complex link between riches and happiness.

The Illusion of Happiness: It's a widespread misconception that acquiring riches will make you happy. In our ideal world, having enough money brings endless delight. But reality frequently has a different narrative. Although money can buy us comfort and momentary joys, it lacks the alchemical ability to alter our inner condition of happiness. The delusion that acquiring riches will make you happier is strong and persistent.

Genuine happiness is a multifaceted diamond that draws from sources other than worldly goods. Happiness goes beyond worldly wealth. It comes from the caliber of our connections, our sense of direction, and our personal development. These are the things that really make our lives richer, and riches alone cannot buy them.

The importance of perspective: How we respond to the world around us affects how happy we feel. The excitement of obtaining a brand-new item or going on a brand-new excursion sometimes wears off with time. This phenomenon, sometimes referred to as the hedonic treadmill, shows that continuous happiness calls for more than a relentless pursuit of monetary success.

The Search for Balance: Being aware of the contradiction between happiness and money motivates us to look for balance. It encourages us to invest in the relationships, experiences, and personal development that lead to long-lasting enjoyment in addition to financial comforts. It serves as a reminder that genuine riches include the diversity of satisfaction within.

The Cost of Extra

Money is a symbol of prosperity, but it also contains a subliminal warning about the dangers of excess. Even if it may appear desirable, excessive money can provide a number of difficulties and complications that require our attention.

The Stress of Consumerism: The desire for excessive affluence drives the quest for more, which can cause stress and worry. The endless cycle of materialism, the need for the newest items, and the stress of trying to live up to cultural ideals place a heavy strain on the mind.

Relationship Stress: Abundant riches can cause relationship stress. Personal relationships may suffer when financial achievement takes precedence. As priorities change, friendships and family relationships may be put to the test, which can result in isolation and estrangement.

The Emptiness of Accumulation: Beyond a certain point, the benefits of amassing material goods frequently start to decline. Eventually, the joy of obtaining new things gives way to a feeling of emptiness. It becomes clear that material goods do not guarantee a happy existence.

The chase for riches can occasionally cast a shadow over the pursuit of purpose. People could become aimless and lose all sense of purpose in their lives when achieving financial success becomes the only goal.

The Priceless Asset that is Time

One of the paradoxes of money's power stands out clearly among the others: money cannot buy time. Time, the most valuable and unrecoverable resource, is nevertheless out of reach for those without financial resources.

Time is sometimes referred to as the greatest treasure since it is an immeasurable asset that cannot be purchased with money. A moment cannot be recovered after it has passed. This insight emphasizes how crucial it is to make the most of each moment, enjoy each one, and build lasting memories.

Time Poverty: In certain circumstances, the unrelenting quest for financial achievement results in a type of poverty known as time poverty. People could find themselves continuously preoccupied with duties or work, which leaves little time for fun, rest, or spending time with loved ones.

Achieving a healthy balance between work and play, business and personal life, is crucial for making the most use of your time. It recognizes that the quality of life is not exclusively determined by financial success but also by the moments we cherish and the connections we cultivate.

Beyond Material Wealth: The True Riches

We come to the deep realization that genuine prosperity goes beyond the domain of tangible belongings as we negotiate the dual currency of money. It includes an immense wealth of love, connections, personal development, and purpose.

Money can make it easier to meet people and participate in activities, but money cannot be used to buy true love, trust, or lasting friendships. Shared experiences, emotional ties, and the dedication of time and energy are the foundations of authentic partnerships.

Personal Development: A crucial component of real riches is the process of personal development and self-discovery. It's a road that incorporates the quest for knowledge, wisdom, and a better understanding of oneself and goes beyond the limitations of material prosperity.

Purpose and satisfaction: A feeling of purpose and satisfaction is the foundation of true prosperity. It is the knowledge that achieving one's potential, pursuing passions, and making a difference in the world are what give life its purpose.

The Legacy of Impact: An enduring type of wealth is the mark we leave on the world and the improvements we bring about in other people's lives. It endures as a reminder of our ideals and contributions and transcends material goods.

Advice from Those Who Have Been There

We look to the experience of those who have traveled through its many turns and turns to bring our voyage through the intricate tapestry of riches and well-being to a close. Their experiences and perceptions provide insightful guidance for negotiating the complex link between wealth and quality of life.

Advice from the wise philosophers, intellectuals, and those who have tasted the highs and lows of riches has left us with wisdom that endures through the centuries. They serve as a reminder that while money is a useful instrument, its ultimate effect is found in how we utilize it to improve both our own and other people's quality of life.

Balancing the Scales: The Way to True Wealth

We consider the lessons we've learned and the contradictions we've solved as our investigation comes to a close. We stress the significance of aiming for a positive relationship with money—one that recognizes its potential and constraints. Money can improve our lives, but it cannot take the place of the intangible values of love, relationships, personal development, and purpose.

We find a balanced existence that embraces the whole range of human experience when we pursue genuine prosperity. In this life, pursuing pleasure and financial security go hand in hand, and the richness of life is evaluated not just by material goods but also by moments, connections, and the imprint we leave on the world.

Understanding the dual nature of money gives us a profound insight into the complexity of life's endeavors. It's an invitation to go out on a voyage that goes beyond the bounds of material prosperity and explores the infinite riches of the human experience—a journey where the actual treasures are discovered in the eternal, priceless, and immeasurable things.

Understanding What Money Can and Can't Buy: The Enchanted Coin

There was a fascinating young woman named Emily who lived in a little, ancient town tucked away amid the hills. Emily had always been intrigued by life's mysteries, but one in particular had captivated her attention: What could money purchase, and what lay beyond its purview? Emily came upon an elderly guy with a weathered face and a glint in his eye as she was strolling through the busy marketplace one bright morning. He was seated in front of a rickety wooden cart filled with various antiques and oddities. The centerpiece of his collection was a coin that Emily had never seen before. It had an ethereal sheen about it and shimmered as if it had been touched by magic. Emily approached the elderly guy and asked him about the coin out of curiosity. He told her a story that would inspire her to try to figure out what money could and couldn't buy, with a knowing smile. ***The Enchanted Coin: A Fairy Tale The mythology of the charmed coin***, whose owner was thought to be able to fulfill any material wish, is where the old man's tale began. The elderly guy was describing the coin's astounding abilities, and Emily was listening intently. It allowed one to purchase the largest homes, the most beautiful feasts, and the greatest jewelry. Emily traded the charmed coin for some of her own to experience its enchantment firsthand. She couldn't resist the temptation of having a way to have all she wanted materially. The first stop on Emily's travels was an opulent home perched on a hill. The mansion appeared before her eyes with a flip of the coin, beyond her wildest expectations with its sumptuous beauty. She also yearned for a wardrobe stocked with the most expensive clothing. Her closet quickly filled to the brim with pearls, jewels, and silks. However, Emily began to feel a gnawing emptiness in her heart as the days stretched into weeks. The once-safe home seemed chilly and enveloping. The magnificent clothing, which had previously been a thrill, now appeared heavy. She now feels deprived after the magical feast that tasted so good.

Emily found the elderly man again, this time puzzled and discouraged, and gave him the magical coin back. What can money buy, and what remains untouched by it? she pondered as she expressed her disillusionment. The elderly man said, "Money may buy houses, clothes, and feasts, but it cannot purchase the comfort of a tranquil heart, the warmth of a loving hug, or the laughter of genuine friendship. Although money can enrich your life materially, it cannot satisfy the emptiness in your spirit.

Epiphany of Emily

Emily stepped out of the old man's wagon with fresh comprehension. While money might purchase comfort and security, she realized that these things couldn't replace the intangible values that genuinely filled life. All of these things were beyond the grasp of any charmed currency, including love, joy, compassion, and purpose. With this insight, Emily set off on a new journey, one that emphasized friendships, adventures, and the quest for a fulfilling existence. She came to realize that the richest things in life are not the things that accumulate; rather, they are the riches of the human spirit. As the years went by, Emily's life developed into a tapestry woven with occasions of love, joy, and purpose. She loved the simple joys of good company, the splendor of dawn, and the satisfaction of assisting others. By solving the riddle of what money could and could not purchase, she discovered a treasure that was worth much more than any magical coin. Thus, Emily's story serves as a timeless reminder that, even though money may buy a lot of things, it cannot buy the essence of a happy and fulfilling life. Happiness, meaning, or a profound human connection cannot be purchased. The intangible experiences and connections that feed the spirit are where real richness in life may be found. It's important to keep in mind that, while money has its role, it is not the only factor in determining our value or pleasure as we go through our financial adventures. Compassion, empathy, love, and purpose are among the things that cannot be purchased with money; by putting these first, we may find the genuine treasures that make life truly enthralling. The enchantment we discover in the world around us and inside ourselves ultimately matters more than the magical currency we amass.

Chapter 2

The Stories We Tell - How Money Narratives Shape Our Choices

The mysterious stories we tell ourselves about money that influence how we view and deal with riches are the unseen conductors of our financial lives. Imagine them as the subconscious scripts, frequently buried deep within our thoughts, that choreograph the complex dance of our financial decisions. These narratives are the tales we tell ourselves about money, tales that serve as the foundation for our attitudes, beliefs, and actions. They may be enticing or ominous, whispering questions about scarcity and restriction or urging us to embrace riches as a weapon for achieving our goals. We are acting out the scenes of these storylines with every salary, investment, and impulsive buy, shaping the tale of our financial journey.

The Art of Influence: Subtle

These financial tales are the silent puppet masters controlling our choices at the level of our conscious awareness. They control how we make financial decisions, creating uncertainty or trust in our choices. Our deeply established financial narratives frequently pull at the strings, influencing our decisions to be prudent rather than indulgent. Similar to this, these tales subtly force our hands when we choose to put money into our future rather than waste it. It's time to expose these puppet masters, acknowledge their ubiquitous influence, and take back control of the narrative as the writers and directors of our financial tale.

Untold Generational Stories

The tales we ingest from our families and societies are potent dramas that continue to influence our decisions in the vast theater of riches. Some of us may be influenced by stories passed down from ancestors who struggled with money that teach us to be prudent and frugal. Others can become snared by tales of luxury and financial irresponsibility, tales spun by societies that associate success with extravagant expenditure. These stories are frequently told from generation to generation, whispered from parent to child, and ingrained in our financial psyche.

It's time for us to pick up a pen and construct stories that resonate with our own aims and ideals, just as every great playwright updates their screenplay to reflect the passing of time and shifting viewpoints. Although the experiences of our ancestors can teach us important lessons, they do not have to determine our future financial success. We have the power to shape our own stories and create a financial narrative that reflects our unique personalities and aspirations.

The Chronicles of Empowerment's composition

It's time to change the plot and take control of our financial story. We might assume the roles of author and director instead of being receptive characters in the stories that have been passed down to us. Let's write stories about how to be financially resilient in the face of hardship, stories about how to overcome our prior constraints, and stories about how to achieve purpose-driven riches. By rewriting our financial tales, we take control of our financial destinies and create narratives that lead us to success, financial freedom, and a life that is enhanced by the pursuit of meaning rather than just gain.

Rewriting these stories requires reexamining our attitudes and assumptions about money. We must consider if our present aims and desires are served by the reasons, we maintain particular financial ideas. It's time to update a money story if it no longer reflects our values or the financial results we want. For instance, if we have been taught that money is limited and must be saved at all costs, we may change our mindset to one of plenty and promote prudent spending and wise investment.

Accepting the Unseen Impact

Money stories are more than just stories; they are the designers of our financial destinies. They murmur in the background while we choose how much to save, spend, and invest. They are the hidden influences that shape our financial habits by influencing our views toward risk and opportunity. The first step in taking back control of our financial decisions is realizing the significant influence of these myths.

How we address financial issues is influenced by our personal money tales. In the case of financial uncertainty, for example, if we have a scarcity mindset, we could feel fearful and risk-averse. People who have stories of prosperity, on the other hand, could see these difficulties as chances for development and creativity.

Additionally, these stories influence how we see happiness and success. We may put financial gain ahead of other parts of life if we think that acquiring riches is the best indicator of success and pleasure. In doing so, we run the risk of jeopardizing our health, relationships, and general well-being. On the other hand, those whose stories emphasize overall wellbeing could try to strike a balance between material achievement and personal fulfillment.

Our financial situation has a tangible impact on how we make decisions. They have an impact on our spending patterns, financial objectives, investment choices, and even our job selections. For instance, someone who prioritizes financial stability could emphasize retirement savings, whereas someone who prioritizes instant satisfaction might focus spending on transient pleasures.

Selecting fresh narratives

We may select money narratives that will enable us to make wiser financial decisions if we are aware of their effects. It's about realizing that, despite the fact that these narratives may have been influenced by our early experiences and upbringing, we have the ability to change them in order to make them more consistent with our present aspirations and objectives.

To start this revolutionary process, take some time to consider your present financial circumstances. What attitudes and convictions do you have towards money? Are they restricting or empowering? What impact do they have on your financial decisions?

Challenge Your Beliefs: Examine your attitudes about money. Consider the reasons behind your convictions and whether they support your morals and financial objectives.

Creating New Narratives: Write new stories that reflect the financial results you want to achieve. You should be motivated and inspired to make wiser financial decisions by these stories.

Seeking Support: Talk to dependable friends, family members, or financial advisers who can offer advice and hold you accountable for your new narratives.

Consistent Practice: Through daily affirmations or visualizations, repeatedly reinforce your new narratives. These stories will gradually permeate your brain and influence how you behave financially.

The tales we tell ourselves about money are major plotlines in the broad story of our lives. They influence our wealth-related attitudes, actions, and beliefs, which in turn affect how we fare financially. We may take charge of our financial destinies by realizing the influence of these storylines. We may successfully traverse the complicated world of money by updating and creating new narratives that enable us to make wiser financial decisions. Our stories serve as the compass for this trip, pointing us in the direction of financial success and a life enhanced by the search for meaning and satisfaction.

The Tale of Two Narratives: Clara and James' Relationship with Money

James and Clara, two longtime friends, resided in the thriving town of Millville. When it came to their viewpoints on money, they were unlike night and day, and the decisions they made in life reflected the stories they believed about riches.

The security narrative of Clara

Clara was raised in a humble home where having a stable income was very important. Her economical and responsible parents taught her the importance of setting money aside for emergencies. They frequently related tales of the financial struggles they had gone through as children, which had deeply affected little Clara. As Clara became older, security and stability were the main themes in her explanation of money. She thought that having a safety net and a cushion to guard against life's unforeseen storms was a sign of financial success. This idea influenced her decisions. She conscientiously set aside some of her salary, made payments to her retirement account, and accumulated cash reserves. Clara decided to forego some of her career goals to take a job with a stable paycheck. She decided to live simply yet comfortably, prioritizing needs above wants. Clara's story has helped her throughout the years. She handled financial losses gracefully, certain that her thorough preparedness offered a safety net. Her decisions in life reflected her conviction that having financial security was essential.

James' Abundance Narrative

James, on the other hand, was a boyhood friend of Clara's who had a very different perspective on money. His parents were successful business people who amassed their riches over time. They frequently regaled him with tales of invention, taking chances, and the pleasure of monetary triumph. James had a story of riches from a young age. He thought that money was a tool for generating experiences and possibilities. His decisions were a reflection of his ambition for an exciting, opulent life spent pursuing his passions. James invested in businesses he believed in rather than assiduously saving money, occasionally taking calculated risks. He chose to pursue a profession in an area he was enthusiastic about, despite the risk and unclear financial rewards. His extravagant way of life included everything from luxurious travel to good eating. James experienced financial ups and downs, but his belief in plenty strengthened him. He thought that failures were just temporary and that there were many chances to succeed financially. His decisions in life demonstrated his readiness to take chances to achieve his goals.

Interaction of Narratives

Their financial storylines continued to influence Clara and James' decisions as they hit their middle ages.

Clara took solace in the fact that her meticulous preparation had guaranteed her retirement and given her a sense of security. She treasured the peace of mind her story of security had given her, loved simple pleasures, and respected her close-knit neighborhood. James, on the other hand, has gone through both successful and unsuccessful financial periods. He toured the globe, embraced his hobbies with unrelenting devotion, and delighted in the thrill of business endeavors. He had traveled a journey marked by hardships and victories, thanks to his tale of prosperity. One day, Clara and James discussed their life decisions over a cup of tea at the small café in Millville. Clara was in awe of James' risk-taking activities and spirit of exploration. James respected Clara's financial stability and knowledge. They came to see that the stories they had been telling themselves about money had influenced not only their financial outcomes but also their values and priorities.

Making sense of our financial decisions

Longtime friends Clara and James, who had quite different financial histories, learned that there wasn't a single, universal method of handling money. Their stories showed how our views about money, whether they are based on security or plenty, affect the decisions we make in life. We may make decisions that are in line with our beliefs and objectives by understanding our own financial stories. It's not a matter of choosing one story over another, but rather of understanding how the two interact and striking a balance that results in a happy and successful life. Clara and James discovered in the community of Millville that their financial stories were like the hues on an artist's palette, each adding to the lovely picture of their lives. The secret was to depict a life that satisfied their genuine goals, whether that meant accepting wealth, security, or a peaceful coexistence of the two.

Chapter 3

The Growth of Money Over Time – Unveiling the Magic of Compound Interest

Money has the capacity to increase through time, giving it a special and transforming power. Compound interest, a fundamental financial concept, is what causes this occurrence, instead of alchemy or mysticism. A secret garden of riches where the seeds we sow now might thrive into a plentiful financial harvest in the future can be compared to when we understand how money grows through time.

The First Invested Dollar

Consider cash as a seed. You are effectively putting this seed in the fertile soil of the financial market when you invest it, whether it be in a savings account, stocks, bonds, or other financial instruments. This seed has the capacity to grow thanks to the idea of compound interest rather than through the use of magic.

Compound Interest's Magic

The financial analog of a snowball effect is compound interest. It's the mechanism by which the interest on your money generates further interest. Over time, this compounding may turn modest, consistent investments into considerable riches.

This is how it goes

Consider making a $1,000 investment with a 5% yearly interest rate. You would accrue $50 in interest throughout the first year, increasing your total to $1,050. Now, in the second year, that 5% interest applies to both the $50 you made in the first year and the $1,000 you initially invested. In the second year, you would thus get $52.50 in interest, raising your total to $1,102.50. This cycle keeps on, and as time goes on, your money starts to rise faster.

Time and patience have great power

The role of time itself is one of the most astounding elements of how money has grown over time. The results grow more significant the longer you let your money multiply. It's like witnessing a tiny seed develop into a strong oak tree in terms of money.

Take the cases of Alex and Ben as two examples. Alex begins investing $1,000 a year at the age of 25 and keeps doing so until the age of 35, making a total contribution of $10,000. Ben, on the other hand, starts investing $1,000 a year at the age of 35 and keeps doing so until he is 65, making a total contribution of $30,000. By the time Alex is 65, his assets will have increased to around

$177,000, assuming an average yearly return of 7%. In comparison, despite investing three times as much money, Ben's assets will only increase in value by around $147,000. The impact of compound interest and the additional time Alex's assets had to develop are to blame for this startling discrepancy.

Risk and Benefit

While compound interest may do wonders for your finances, it is vital to remember that there are certain risks involved. The risk associated with various investments varies, and bigger potential profits are frequently coupled with more volatility. For instance, historically, stocks have outperformed bonds or savings accounts in terms of long-term returns, but their short-term volatility is higher.

In the realm of wealth creation, knowing your risk tolerance and diversifying your assets are essential. Spreading your assets over a variety of asset types helps lower risk. Using this method, you can weather market downturns and continue to reap the rewards of your investments' long-term development potential.

The value of consistent donations

Another important element in maximizing the long-term growth potential of money is consistency. Compound interest works in your favor when you consistently make investments. If you regularly contribute to your assets, such as by setting up automatic payments to your retirement account, the compounding engine will have more gasoline.

Accounts that are tax-favored

Governments in many nations provide tax-advantaged retirement accounts as an incentive to save for the future. These accounts, which include 401(k)s and IRAs in the US, offer tax advantages that can accelerate your money's growth over time. The growth within these accounts is tax-deferred until withdrawal, allowing your investments to compound more effectively. Frequently, contributions to these accounts are tax-deductible.

Influence of Inflation

While compound interest might accelerate your financial growth, it's critical to take inflation into account. Over time, inflation reduces the purchasing power of your money, resulting in a decrease in what the same amount of money can purchase. It's critical to look for assets that have the ability to outperform inflation and maintain the real worth of your money to fend against the ravages of inflation.

Taking Care of the Garden of Wealth

Money doesn't increase over time by accident or luck; it grows over time as a result of a well-known financial theory that may be used to your advantage if you have the correct investing strategy, patience, and persistence. Compound interest may help you turn little, regular contributions into sizable riches, whether you're saving for retirement, school, or other long-term goals. You may tend to your financial garden, seeing your money develop and thrive over time, much like a gardener tends to their garden, nourishing it with care and attention. The possibilities for your financial future are endless when you use compound interest as your secret weapon and time as your ally.

The Enchanted Garden: Revealing Compound Interest's Magic

A little girl named Lily lived in a small village that was perched on the edge of a vast forest. Lily was well known for having an endless supply of questions. She frequently stumbled into the woods in search of solutions to life's puzzles. She discovered a secret garden one bright day that had a profound secret about compound interest that would transform her life forever.

The Secret Garden

Lily discovered a variety of plants and trees as she strolled around the garden, each one more beautiful than the previous. A majestic oak tree with upward-extending branches stood in the middle of the garden. A body of water underneath it mirrored the brilliant blue of the sky. This enchanted garden was cared for by Mr. Anderson, a knowledgeable old gardener. He invited Lily to relax by the pool after spotting her interest. He started to reveal the mystery of the garden with a glint in his eye.
"Lily," Mr. Anderson remarked, "this garden embodies the concept of compound interest—a force of nature as powerful as the growth of these plants."

The Foundations of Wealth

A little seed was taken out of Mr. Anderson's pocket and placed in the fertile soil. He clarified that this seed was for an initial financial investment or quantity of money. It would develop into a tree of riches given the correct circumstances, such as rich soil and tender care.
He said, "Just as a seed planted in the fertile ground grows into a towering tree, your initial investment, when allowed to grow undisturbed, can yield tremendous returns over time."

The capacity for growth

Lily marveled as Mr. Anderson went on. But when you allow the money tree to grow fruit, the true magic happens. The fruits themselves carry seeds, which cause the riches to grow rapidly. He gave an example by sowing another tree seed in the ground. "Look at how this fresh seed is growing next to the old one. It will eventually start to produce its fruits, starting a cycle of growth that becomes stronger every year. Lily became more aware of the serious ramifications, and her eyes widened. The tree may grow bigger and more profitable if it is left alone to develop and the profits are reinvested, right? Mr. Anderson smiled sagely and nodded. Indeed, my darling. This is compound interest's alluring power. It matters how intelligently you tend to your financial garden, not simply how much money you start with.

The Timeless Lesson

Lily kept going to the enchanted garden as the seasons changed. She discovered that the most important component in the compound interest formula is time. The harvest would be more plentiful the longer they allowed their investments to develop. The key, as Mr. Anderson underlined, is patience. It takes time for your investments to realize their full potential, just as it does for a sapling to develop into a strong tree. Lily took this lesson to heart and understood that the key to compound interest's power lay in persistent saving and thoughtful investing decisions.

The Prosperous Harvest

After some time had passed, Lily, who was now a young lady, managed her finances. She carefully managed her assets, saw the growth of her funds, and let compound interest do its miracles.

Her early investments were successful, and she reinvested the profits to continue the cycle of development that the magical garden represented. Her riches increased year after year, as Mr. Anderson had predicted. Lily's financial garden came to represent her perseverance and commitment. She realized that the magic of compound interest wasn't just a concept found in fairy tales but rather a real power that anybody with the correct training and commitment could master.

Bringing the Enchantment to Light

The power of compound interest—a force that might gradually turn small money into substantial wealth—was shown through Lily's travels. She taught people in her neighborhood how to grow their financial gardens and reap the benefits of patient investment by sharing her expertise. In the end, Lily and her town learned a priceless lesson from the magical garden and its compound interest secret: that with patience, consideration, and wise financial decisions, even the smallest seed of riches might blossom into a bountiful forest of prosperity. The potential of compound interest was no longer a closely guarded secret but rather a readily available resource that anybody could use to improve their financial situation.

Chapter 4

Predicting the Future - The Pitfalls of Trying to Forecast Financial Markets

Even the most experienced investors struggle to resist the siren's song of market predictions in the thrilling world of finance. Who wouldn't want to look into the future of finance and predict the rise and fall of stocks, the changes in interest rates, or the twists in the value of different currencies? The idea of possessing a crystal ball that may reveal the secrets of wealth is alluring. The maze of perilous traps and uncertainty that lies behind the attraction of predicting, however, can trap even the most well-intentioned investor.

The Illusion of Complete Certainty

The idea of certainty is the first trap that tempts forecasting enthusiasts. Predictions made by financial gurus or self-styled oracles are frequently presented with an appearance of unchanging assurance. Such assurance might be deceptive and induce false security among investors. It's important to keep in mind that a complex network of events, many of which are unpredictable, affects the financial markets. Certainty is a precious commodity in this world.

The Unpredictability of Markets

Financial markets behave like uncontrolled, untamed animals that are ruled by the irrational whims of a constantly shifting environment. Among the myriad factors that have the power to quickly change market dynamics are economic conditions, geopolitical events, technological advancements, and investor emotion. No matter how experienced the forecaster, trying to predict market movements in the face of such intricacy is comparable to trying to predict a butterfly's flight route in a hurricane.

The Underappreciated Efficient Market Theory

Let's talk about the **Efficient Market Hypothesis** (EMH), a foundational concept in financial theory. It makes the assumption that asset prices already take into account all relevant information and that markets are efficient. It basically says that repeatedly beating the market with predictions is like chasing a phantom. According to the EMH, the prediction game is extremely difficult because any knowledge that could alter prices is quickly assimilated into asset values.

The Human Element: Emotional Fluctuations and Cognitive Biases

Predicting mistakes frequently involves a significant amount of psychology and emotion. Forecasters may interpret data selectively, confirming their forecasts while missing contrary evidence due to cognitive biases such as the well-known overconfidence and confirmation bias. This complex dance involves emotions as well. Long-term financial goals can be harmed by fear and greed, which can impair judgment and lead to rash actions based on forecasts for the near future.

A short-term focus that neglects long-term objectives

The focus of forecasting is frequently on the near future, with predictions of the upcoming market movement, quarter, or year being common. This shortsighted viewpoint may draw attention away from the expansive web of long-term financial goals. An excessive focus on short-term forecasts may result in excessive trading, increased transaction costs, and missed opportunities for compounding's wealth-building miracles.

The High Cost of Being Wrong

Consider the expense of inaccurate forecasting; the repercussions of incorrect predictions might be disastrous. Investors who make decisions based on incorrect estimates run the risk of suffering significant losses, missing out on lucrative possibilities, or being caught in a vicious cycle of buying high and selling low, which can lead to bankruptcy.

Time in the market versus market timing

Missed chances are frequently the outcome of the never-ending pursuit of market timing, a tactic predicated on the illusive objective of buying low and selling high. Reputable investors have often emphasized the value of "time in the market" rather than "timing the market." Long-term investing often yields better outcomes than attempting to foresee quick changes in the market.

Groupthink's danger and the expert consensus

Even expert consensus is vulnerable to forecasting's dangers. According to studies, financial forecasters and experts frequently predict the wrong things, and their forecasts don't always outperform the market. Relying only on forecasts from experts might be deceptive and may not result in better investment results.

Finding Your Way Through Finance's Shifting Sands

The siren's lure of market forecasting calls for promises of immeasurable wealth in the seductive world of finance. But beyond the surface, there is a world full of peril and traps. Making wiser and more informed investing decisions requires an understanding of these hazards and their limitations.

Investors can find comfort in strategies that place an emphasis on diversification, long-term planning, and risk management rather than trying to forecast the unforeseen. Understanding the forecasting process's limits is an essential first step in navigating the broad and unpredictably changing financial world. The wisdom of a steady hand and a long-term perspective is frequently what leads to the most permanent prosperity as we negotiate these shifting sands. The keys to financial success in this complex dance of money are not found in the crystal ball but rather in the virtues of restraint, caution, and a well-thought-out investment plan.

The Pitfalls of Predicting Financial Markets: The Fortuneteller's Folly

Madam Zara, the town's well-known fortuneteller, was a strange person who resided in the busy town of Prospera. Madam Zara appeared to have a remarkable capacity for prophecy. People consulted her for advice on topics of love, health, and, of course, financial markets from all over the world.

A young man called David, who was inquisitive, went to see Madam Zara one bright afternoon. He was anxious to learn more about her industry insights after hearing stories about her amazing forecasts. David thought he could gain enormous money if he could see into the future of the markets.

The Conversation with Mrs. Zara

David was greeted by Madam Zara in her gloomy salon, which was decorated with a variety of magical items. She pointed to her crystal ball, where she claimed to be able to predict the future, and motioned for him to sit.

David inquired, "Madam Zara, can you tell me which stocks will soar in the coming months?" His pulse was thumping with expectation. I want to ensure my financial future by making smart investments.

Madam Zara briefly closed her eyes before speaking in a low, mysterious voice. "I see a wild sea and a rising sun. I saw both riches made and lost. However, my darling, the details are still obscured by ambiguity.

She continued by saying that while she could give broad insights into market patterns, she was unable to anticipate precise stock moves. She stressed that the direction of the financial markets was as erratic as the winds that blow over the ocean.

David's Prediction Addiction

David was unfazed and got obsessed with the notion of forecasting the financial markets. He stayed up late reading financial news, reviewing graphs, and examining any market signal he could get his hands on. He followed seasoned experts, signed up for newsletters, and even experimented with intricate financial models.

David became more and more preoccupied with forecasts as time went on. He made rash financial choices based on the most recent forecasts, frequently buying high and selling low in an ineffectual effort to track the market's illusive future.

Pitfalls Identified

David's pursuit of market forecasts sent him down a perilous path as months went into years. He started to see that the markets were becoming more unpredictable as he tried to predict them. The markets appeared to have a mind of their own, despite his best efforts to predict their movements.

He saw market shocks that no one had anticipated, economic crises that came on suddenly, and expert predictions that failed. The expenses associated with regular trading and the emotional cost of following market predictions caused David's once-promising portfolio to decline.

Astonishing Revelation

In the middle of yet another financial slump, David ran into Sarah, an old friend. She had adopted a new strategy for investing, one that relied on long-term, diversified techniques rather than forecasting the future.

Sarah discussed her views with me over a cup of coffee. "David," she added, "trying to foresee the financial markets is like attempting to predict the weather months in advance. It's a pointless activity. Instead, I focus my attention on diversifying my holdings, making long-term investments, and maintaining discipline despite market fluctuations.

David paid close attention as she spoke, recognizing how wise she was. He realized Madam Zara's enigmatic message had been deeper than he had previously believed. Indeed, it was foolish to attempt to anticipate the financial markets since they were as unpredictable as a rough sea.

The Fortuneteller's Lesson, in summary

David's experience served as a sad lesson on the difficulties of making financial market predictions. His preoccupation with making forecasts had cost him personally and financially. Finally, he agreed with Sarah's idea, realizing that even if the markets were volatile, a well-planned, long-term investment strategy could weather the storms and provide positive financial results.

David departed the field of market forecasting with the humble knowledge that certain things, like the direction of financial markets, were better left to the enigmas of time. The markets' future remained unpredictable, as Madam Zara had warned, and disciplined, patient investing—rather than the fruitless chase of fortune-telling—represented the real road to riches.

Chapter 5

Luck and Skill - Understanding the Role of Luck in Financial Success

These two words, **"financial success,"** frequently evoke thoughts of riches, prosperity, and an abundant existence. Many of us work hard for it, making wise financial decisions and creating future plans. But chance is a subtle and sometimes ignored aspect that operates in addition to hard work and wise decision-making. The results of our efforts can be greatly shaped by luck, both good and bad, in ways we may not always be aware of. In this thorough investigation, we go in-depth to comprehend the complex role that luck plays in achieving financial success, looking at its effects, psychological components, and strategies for navigating its choppy waters.

I. *The Difficult Dance of Chance and Work*

There is a complicated and frequently unclear interplay at the core of the luck and financial success connection. It takes a sophisticated viewpoint to comprehend this relationship—one that recognizes the contributions of both chance and effort.

- *The Value of Effort*

Every success story is built on effort and the sweat equity we put into our financial endeavors. It's the years of commitment to school, the late hours at work, and the discipline to save money and make sensible investments. Our capacity to make wise judgments, establish objectives, and work assiduously to achieve them is what we refer to as effort. It is an aspect of the equation that is under our control and a crucial factor in achieving financial success.

- *The Mysterious Character of Luck*

Contrarily, luck is the wildcard, the unpredictability that has the power to either increase or decrease the results of our efforts. It covers a broad range, from positive happenings like winning the lottery or discovering a profitable investment to bad occurrences like a sudden health crisis or economic depression. By its very nature, luck is unpredictable and can come at any time, changing the course of our financial future in unexpected ways.

- *The Meeting Point of Effort and Chance*

Success in business frequently results from a combination of work and good fortune. It's the intersection of opportunity and careful planning, of years of toil and a lucky break. Even though we have little control over chance, we may put ourselves in a position to maximize the benefits of lucky situations and minimize the repercussions of unfavorable ones. This necessitates careful planning, risk management, and adaptability in combination.

II. *How Luck Affects Financial Success*

Understanding the function of luck has real ramifications for our financial well-being and goes beyond philosophical reflection.

- ### *Good Fortune: Windfalls and Chances*

Positive luck, the sort that results in unanticipated benefits or chances, may propel us toward monetary achievement. This could take the form of a timely bequest, a wise investment, or a happy accident that results in a successful business collaboration. Positive luck may greatly speed up our development, transforming years of work into success that seems to happen suddenly.

- ### *Bad Luck: Obstacles and Setbacks*

Negative fortune, on the other hand, brings difficulties that may impede our financial progress. Unexpected medical costs, losing our jobs during a recession, or making a bad investment can all cause us to fall behind dramatically. Negative luck may negate the progress earned through hard work and thoughtful preparation; therefore, resilience and adaptation are required to manage its effects.

- ***The Incorrect Assessment of Success and Failure***

The mistaken attribution of results is one of the psychological elements of luck's influence on financial success. We frequently minimize the importance of chance when success comes our way by attributing it exclusively to our efforts. On the other hand, when we experience failures, we can be eager to attribute them to other forces, such as poor luck. This cognitive bias can result in excessive self-criticism while facing problems and overconfidence when things are going well.

III. *The psychological aspects of luck in financial success*

Investigating the psychological factors that influence our perceptions, choices, and financial actions is essential to comprehending the significance of luck.

- ***Survival Bias***

A cognitive bias called "survival bias" causes us to frequently ignore the importance of chance. It happens when we highlight the triumphs of those who have overcome hardship and attained financial prosperity. We focus on the survivors but ignore the numerous others who encountered the same difficulties yet failed due to unfavorable luck. This prejudice could perpetuate the idea that hard work alone ensures success.

- ***The Luck-Effort Equilibrium***

It takes skill to psychologically strike a balance between acknowledging good fortune and acknowledging hard work. If people place too much stock in luck, they may develop a fatalistic mindset and believe that they have little control over their financial future. On the other hand, putting too much emphasis on work alone can lead to arrogance and overconfidence. Achieving a good balance requires accepting both chance and work, which enables us to make wise judgments and efficiently manage risk.

- ***Perceived Control and Its Function***

A key psychological aspect is perceived control, or the conviction that we can affect the course of events. It may have an impact on our readiness to take chances, our capacity to bounce back from failures, and our general financial health. We may develop humility and resiliency by realizing that luck is outside of our control; these traits will aid us in navigating the ups and downs of our financial path.

IV. *Dealing with Luck's Unpredictability*

How can we successfully traverse the choppy waters of financial success given the crucial role that luck plays?

- ***Risk Management and Prudent Planning***

Prudent financial planning requires putting together plans for both anticipated and unforeseen events. To lessen the effects of bad luck, it is important to diversify investments, accumulate an emergency fund, and get insurance. Furthermore, establishing reasonable budgets and goals might support coordinating our activities with our financial goals.

- ***Flexibility and Robustness***

In a world where luck plays a big part, developing flexibility and resilience is essential. A potent tool for handling financial difficulties is the capacity to modify our methods and expectations in response to shifting circumstances. We may overcome failures and carry on with our path to financial achievement by having resilience.

- ***Thankfulness and Humility***

Understanding the significance of luck fosters thankfulness and modesty. Gratitude enables us to recognize the fortunate coincidences that have formed our financial journey, while humility teaches us that success is not exclusively a product of our efforts. Independent of our financial situation, showing appreciation can promote satisfaction and wellbeing.

- ***Seeking Expert Guidance***

Financial consultants can offer insightful advice on how to handle chance's element of unpredictability. They may aid in risk assessment, investment diversification, and the development of financial strategies that are in line with our objectives and risk tolerance. In the face of both good and terrible fortune, a financial counselor may be a reliable source of reasonable perspective and assist us in making wise decisions.

V. *Concluding Statement: A Fair View*

Understanding the complex role luck plays in achieving financial success is a journey that calls for a balanced viewpoint. It acknowledges that while hard work is a key factor in success, luck may also have a significant impact on our financial destiny. Accepting this complexity can help you make better decisions, be more flexible, and have a deeper understanding of the uncertain path to financial success. Luck and effort are entwined threads in the big fabric of our financial life, and it is in their delicate dance that we discover both obstacles and chances, failures and victories, and, eventually, the realization of our financial goals.

The Winds of Luck: Alice's Adventure in Financial Navigation

Once upon a time, a woman by the name of Alice lived in a peaceful suburban area. Alice was well-known for having sound financial advice. She had methodically saved, invested, and planned for her future for years. She was always ready to share her knowledge and was frequently asked for financial advice by her friends and neighbors.

Discipline and diligence have been hallmarks of Alice's financial journey. She had dutifully set up a percentage of her salary, made prudent investments in a diverse portfolio, and resisted the seductive call of reckless spending. She took satisfaction in her ability to make intelligent judgments and in the steady growth of her money over the years.

One bright morning, while Alice sipped her coffee and looked over her financial portfolio, a neighbor called Bob excitedly approached her.

Bob yelled, "Alice, I've found a fantastic investment opportunity! It's a fledgling firm with ground-breaking technology, and I have a hunch its stock will soar. I'll give it my best.

Alice arched an eyebrow, ever the cautious investor. She was aware of the dangers of investing in startups and the fact that the path to financial success was frequently paved with the remains of failed businesses.

"Bob," Alice said, "although it's true that certain businesses may generate amazing rewards, they also come with a significant amount of risk. Have you done extensive research on this business? Do you know what sector it belongs to? What will you do if things don't turn out the way you want them to?

Bob smiled scornfully and dismissed her worries. "Alice, I get a positive vibe about this. In addition, I've been experiencing a run of fortunate events lately—a few scratch-off lottery wins, some unanticipated bonuses at work. Luck is on my side!"

Alice nodded, her knowledge of the erratic nature of luck serving as a reminder. She realized that while luck may occasionally result in windfalls, it could also be erratic and unpredictable.

As the months passed, Alice maintained a careful approach to portfolio management by maintaining a focus on risk management and diversification. Bob, on the other hand, invested a sizable percentage of his funds in the start-up business he thought would help him achieve his financial goals.

Then, on a pivotal day, word reached the financial world that the fledgling business Bob had invested in had declared bankruptcy, shocking everyone. The innovative technology had encountered unanticipated difficulties, and the company's stock had nearly lost all of its value.

Bob was in shock. He had staked a significant portion of his financial future, and the stars had turned against him. He was now dealing with significant losses as a result of his rash choice to invest on the basis of a lucky run.

While all was going on, Alice observed with a combination of sympathy and apprehension. She was aware that achieving financial success required more than just good fortune or hard work. Finding a happy medium between the two involved accepting the importance of chance while still making wise decisions based on study, preparation, and discipline.

Following the failure of the startup, Bob went to Alice for advice. She worked with him to determine his financial condition, create a strategy to replenish his funds, and diversify his holdings to reduce risk. Together, they mapped out Bob's financial future in a way that was more balanced and took into account the value of both work and the erratic forces of luck.

The tale of Alice and Bob should serve as a warning that achieving financial success is a difficult journey. It's important to put in effort, discipline, and make wise decisions, but it's also important to recognize that luck, both good and bad, may have a big impact on our financial lives. We may maximize our possibilities and withstand any storms that fortune may bring by navigating this complex dance with humility and caution.

Chapter 6

Navigating the Financial Maze - Dealing with Risk and Uncertainty in Finances

The single thing that never changes in the world of finance. The actions and consequences of both individuals and corporations are significantly influenced by the dynamics of risk and uncertainty in this area. One must not only comprehend these dynamics to successfully traverse this complex environment but also adopt techniques that transform risk and uncertainty into chances for development and resilience.

Knowing about Risk and Uncertainty

Although risk and uncertainty are frequently used synonymously, they refer to different concepts in the financial industry:

Risk: Risk may be measured and quantified. It speaks to the possibility and size of a bad thing happening, such as a market slump or an investment loss. Through thorough research, diversification, and risk assessment approaches, risk may be managed.

Uncertainty: On the other hand, uncertainty is less measurable and results from missing or unpredictable knowledge. It includes unanticipated changes in financial markets, occurrences in the economy, and geopolitical variables that can affect financial results. Although uncertainty cannot be completely removed, it may be reduced through planning and flexibility.

Techniques for Handling Risk and Uncertainty

Diversification: Diversification is one of the best methods to control risk. Investors can lessen the effects of subpar performance in any one investment by spreading their assets across several asset classes, sectors, and geographical areas. While diversification does not completely remove risk, it does lessen the impact when a particular industry or asset performs poorly.

Risk Assessment: It's important to comprehend the precise hazards connected with a particular investment. Investors may make wise selections by evaluating aspects including volatility, liquidity, and credit risk. Evaluation of possible outcomes can be aided by resources like risk-reward ratios and stress testing.

Long-Term View: Maintaining a long-term perspective can help people and businesses weather swings and uncertainty in the short term. Despite recurring downturns, historical data indicates that financial markets often increase over time. Long-term benefits can be obtained by sticking to a carefully constructed investing strategy. Building an emergency fund is a sensible way to prepare for unforeseen financial difficulties. Without having to draw on long-term assets, having access to cash can help people get through times of job loss, medical emergencies, or economic downturns.

Continuous Learning: In the world of finance, staying knowledgeable and adaptable is crucial. New financial instruments appear, investment environments shift, and economic conditions do too. Better decision-making is made possible by ongoing learning and staying current on market and financial developments.

Seeking Professional Advice: Financial advisers and specialists may offer insightful advice and support, assisting people and organizations in making decisions that are in line with their financial objectives and risk tolerance. Although they might be frightening, danger and uncertainty also offer chances for advancement and creativity. Businesses that adapt to shifting consumer tastes and market conditions may prosper even in tumultuous times. Investors who practice patience and discipline might take advantage of market turbulence to purchase assets at a discount.

Risk and Uncertainty in Finance: One has to learn more about the nature of risk and uncertainty to fully understand the importance of coping with these two factors in finance.

Risk: The Measurable Force: In the context of finance, risk is the likelihood that a bad thing will happen and the possible severity of its effects. It may frequently be measured quantitatively and evaluated using historical data and statistical analysis. For instance, the risk involved with stock investment is often assessed by looking at variables like price volatility, past performance, and economic indicators. The standard deviation, which indicates the degree of departure from the average return on investment, is a widely used metric for assessing risk. An investment with a larger standard deviation is seen as riskier than one with a smaller one.

Uncertainty: The Improbable Factor: On the other hand, uncertainty results from unpredictable events or insufficient knowledge. It covers things that can't be accurately measured or predicted. Risk can be quantified and controlled to some extent, while uncertainty is, by nature, less controllable. Think about a business that releases a ground-breaking product as an example. Because it depends on several unforeseeable circumstances, including customer responses, competitor responses, and unanticipated market developments, the product launch's success is unclear. Contrary to risk, uncertainty cannot be assessed using previous data or given a specific probability.

The Relationship Between Risk and Uncertainty

Risk and uncertainty frequently interact and intersect in the realm of finance. For instance, exogenous uncertainties like political events or natural disasters might bring an unexpected component, even if an investment may have quantitative risks connected with its previous performance. Developing sensible solutions to deal with financial difficulties requires an understanding of how these factors interact. It necessitates admitting that unforeseen uncertainties might materialize and derail financial strategies even in settings with planned risks.

Techniques for Handling Risk and Uncertainty

In the world of finance, there are countless instances of people and companies dealing with risk and uncertainty, each of which necessitates a different approach to reducing and managing these factors. Spreading risk by diversification is a key element of risk management. Individuals and corporations can lessen the impact of a single investment's underperformance by spreading their assets over a variety of asset types (such as stocks, bonds, and real estate) and geographical areas. For a portfolio's losses to be compensated when one investment underperforms, diversification seeks to make them less linked. For instance, a diversified portfolio's bond value may increase during a stock market slump, providing stability and protecting total wealth.

Assessing Risk: Making Knowledgeable Decisions It is essential to comprehend the precise hazards connected with an investment. Evaluation of different indicators, such as volatility, liquidity, credit risk, and market mood, is part of the risk assessment process. It enables investors to choose wisely based on knowledge about prospective risks and benefits. A framework for assessing whether an investment is fit for one's financial goals and risk tolerance is provided by risk-reward ratios, which evaluate the predicted return of an investment compared to its associated hazards.

Long-Term View: Being Patient in the Face of Uncertainty Having a long-term perspective might help you deal with uncertainty. Financial markets are volatile and unpredictable in the short term, but historical evidence shows that they tend to increase over the long run. Market volatility is frequently best handled by investors who retain a disciplined, long-term attitude.
This point of view encourages people and companies to stick to their investment goals even when things are unclear.

Emergency Fund: A Reserve for Unexpected Events A practical step in preparing for financial instability is to start saving for emergencies. A liquid emergency fund is made up of easily available cash or assets that can cover three to six months' worth of costs. It serves as a safety net for money, acting as a cushion against unanticipated occurrences like job loss, medical crises, or economic downturns. Having an emergency fund enables people to pay for immediate needs without having to withdraw from long-term assets or go into debt during difficult times.

Continuous Learning: being educated Making educated judgments requires being updated about the always-changing financial world. Regulations change, the economy shifts, and new investment possibilities appear. Continuous learning equips people and organizations to adjust to changing conditions, whether via self-study, financial education programs, or expert counsel. Individuals are more equipped to make proactive decisions in the face of uncertainty when they are knowledgeable about financial markets, investing strategies, and risk management measures.

Seeking Professional Counsel: Professional Advice: To help individuals and organizations through the complexity of finance, financial counselors and specialists are crucial. Insights, advice, and custom solutions are offered based on their knowledge. When making difficult financial decisions or long-term goal planning, consulting a professional can be very beneficial. Financial experts assist with determining risk tolerance, building diversified portfolios, and matching assets with specific financial goals.

Seeing Opportunity in Uncertainty

Although they might be frightening, danger and uncertainty also offer chances for advancement and creativity. Businesses that adapt to shifting consumer tastes and market conditions may prosper even in tumultuous times. Investors who practice patience and discipline might take advantage of market turbulence to purchase assets at a discount.

Business Innovation's Function

In the business world, market entrance, product development, and strategic choices are frequently fraught with uncertainty. Successful companies understand that accepting uncertainty may spark innovation and give them a competitive edge. They believe that uncertainty stimulates innovation and flexibility. For instance, a technology business creating a new product is aware of the ambiguity of market demand. The business may launch a minimal viable product (MVP) to obtain input from early consumers rather than waiting for absolute assurance. With this iterative process, they may modify the product depending on feedback from the market, improving their chances of success. When uncertainty is understood and factored into strategic planning, innovation frequently flourishes. Businesses that encourage experimentation and adaptation are typically better equipped to handle sudden changes in the market and new trends.

The Opportunity for Investors Amid Market Volatility

Market volatility, which is frequently a cause for concern, may also offer possibilities for investors. Asset prices may diverge significantly from their fundamental worth when markets go through severe volatility. Investors have the possibility of purchasing undervalued assets as a result of this gap. Take a stock market decline as an illustration. Investors may find it upsetting, but it also presents an opportunity to buy premium equities for less money. Investors that use this "buy low" tactic will profit when the markets ultimately recover. Long-term investors are aware that market volatility is a regular component of the investment process. They could even adjust their portfolios during recurring downturns to make sure that the asset allocations match their investing objectives.

Finding Your Way Through the Financial Maze

Finance risk and uncertainty management is a dynamic process that calls for adaptation, expertise, and a well-structured strategy. It is not a one-size-fits-all undertaking. Effective decision-making is based on knowing the differences between risk and uncertainty. The key strategies for controlling financial risk and uncertainty include diversification, risk assessment, a long-term perspective, emergency savings, continual learning, and expert counsel. These tactics enable people and organizations to make wise decisions, reduce possible drawbacks, and set themselves up for financial success. A mindset that views uncertainty as an opportunity may also foster innovation and expansion in business and investment. The ability to manage the complicated financial environment with greater assurance and transform problems into opportunities on their journey to financial well-being comes from understanding that uncertainty is a normal component of the financial landscape.

The Story of Amelia: Getting Through the Financial Storm

A young woman by the name of Amelia used to reside in the sleepy town of Prosperityville. She was well-known around the world for her bravery and ingenuity. Her experience navigating the rough waters of financial risk and uncertainty offers invaluable advice to anyone pursuing achievement and financial stability.

The Embattled Start

Amelia was reared by diligent parents who emphasized the importance of setting money aside and making plans. They explained to her that there were many uncertainties in life and that being financially prepared was the key to navigating them. Amelia dutifully saved a percentage of her income and created an emergency fund after learning these skills. Amelia's financial caution served her well when she reached maturity. She found a steady job and kept saving, always keeping her long-term objectives in mind. She felt confident about her financial stability and equipped to handle any upcoming uncertainty.

The unexpected obstacle

Suddenly and unexpectedly, a problem arose one tragic day. Prosperityville and its neighboring areas were shaken by the worldwide economic slump. Layoffs were unavoidable since Amelia's workplace, a nearby factory, experienced a severe fall in orders. Amelia was surprised to discover that she was one of those losing their jobs.

Amelia remembered the lessons her parents had taught her about the value of planning as uncertainty hung over her. She had an emergency fund that could pay her bills for several months, providing her with a much-needed safety net during this tough period. However, she was still confronted with tough choices and an unclear financial future.

Accepting Change

Amelia's immediate response to losing her job was anxiety and trepidation. She quickly understood, however, that she could use this time of ambiguity as a springboard for development and transformation. She decided to explore a change in profession in an area for which she had always had a strong passion: sustainability and renewable energy. Although there were difficulties throughout this move, Amelia's tenacity and flexibility helped her navigate the choppy waters of a change of career. She continued her studies and training while using her emergency money to pay for the related expenses.

Prudent Investment

When Amelia's new job started to take shape, she decided to look into investing possibilities. Although she was conscious of the inherent dangers associated with investments, she was also conscious of their potential for long-term gain. She set out on a quest to discover more about the stock market, bonds, and other forms of investing. Amelia approached investing carefully, choosing not to give in to her dread of the unknown. She distributed the risk over a variety of asset classes through her investments, preventing her portfolio from being unduly specialized in any one sector. She continued to have a safety net in the form of her emergency money, which gave her the confidence to make investments.

The Influence of Education and Patience

Amelia's passage through the financial sector was characterized by her patience and dedication to continuing learning. She was aware that the financial markets might fluctuate erratically and beyond her control. She chose a long-term view rather than attempting to time the market or pursue short-term rewards. She kept up her education in the financial markets by going to seminars, reading books, and consulting knowledgeable investors. She was able to make wise judgments and successfully manage the complexity of the financial world because of her commitment to lifelong learning.

Thriving in an Uncertain World

Amelia's profession in sustainability and renewable energy grew throughout the years. Over time, her investments increased gradually, and she grew more financially secure than she had anticipated. She had weathered the storm and flourished despite the difficulties and the unpredictable nature of the voyage.

The life of Amelia is a monument to the value of forethought, adaptation, and toughness in the face of risk and uncertainty. The once-daunting oceans of financial uncertainty were turned into a road of wealth by her capacity to embrace change, make good investments, and retain a long-term perspective.

Conclusion: Getting Through the Financial Storm

Amelia's path through financial risk and uncertainty serves as an example of how problems in life may be used as springboards for development and achievement. People may successfully cross the turbulent waters of financial instability and come out stronger on the other side by creating a strong financial foundation, accepting change, and addressing investments with prudence. The story of Amelia serves as a reminder that while unforeseen uncertainties may occur, being ready and having a resilient attitude may equip people to not just survive but also thrive in the face of difficulty. Others may successfully handle life's financial problems with fortitude, adaptation, and dedication to their long-term goals, just as Amelia did when she discovered her real purpose and financial stability.

Chapter 7

Greed and Fear - How Emotions Impact Our Financial Decisions

Imagine yourself on a rollercoaster; one second, you're ascending to breathtaking heights, and the next you're down at a dizzying rate. The emotional rollercoaster that frequently follows financial decisions, however, is not constructed of steel and rails. Understanding how emotions affect our financial decisions is crucial for making informed judgments and realizing long-term financial objectives since our financial lives include a complicated interaction of logic and feelings.

The Financial Emotional Spectrum

Rarely are financial choices made logically. Emotions significantly affect how we perceive the world and how we make decisions. Here is a sample of the emotional gamut that frequently manifests:

Greed can be brought on by the temptation of immediate financial advantages and riches. To maximize their profits, people may become too risk-averse or make rash investing decisions as a result of this emotion.

Fear: On the other end of the scale, fear is a strong feeling in the financial world. Decision-making might be stymied, and opportunities can be lost as a result of loss anxiety. During market downturns, it can also make people panic, which could lead them to sell their investments at the wrong moment and lock in losses.

Overconfidence: Excessive risk-taking can result from overconfidence. People who feel they have better knowledge or intuition could take on more risk than they can afford because they think they can outwit the situation.

Regret: When financial plans don't work out as planned, regret frequently follows. It may cause uncertainty and second-guessing about upcoming choices, impeding the achievement of financial objectives.

Worry: Concerns about the future, such as job stability, retirement planning, or unforeseen bills, can lead to financial worry. Anxiety might cause people to make overly cautious decisions, such as hoarding money rather than making investments.

Excitation: Excitation and impulsivity can be brought on by favorable financial occurrences, such as obtaining a bonus or inheritance. People could be enticed to spend lavishly or make costly purchases without thinking about the long-term effects.

Emotional Influence on Financial Decisions

It is essential to comprehend the emotional factors that shape our financial decisions. Here is how some of the most prevalent feelings affect financial judgments:

Emotions can cause impulsive purchasing and selling of investments, which can affect investment decisions. When markets are booming, greed may drive people to invest in bubbles, only for them to suffer significant losses when the bubble collapses. In contrast, during market downturns, anxiety can trigger panic selling that results in the lock-up of losses.

Budgeting and Saving: Decisions about budgeting and saving might be influenced by fear and anxiety. People who obsessively worry about probable financial difficulties may hoard money and miss out on investment opportunities. On the other hand, enthusiasm might result in overspending and ignoring financial objectives.

Debt management: Spending due to emotion might result in debt accumulation. Excitement- or instant-gratification-driven impulse purchases might result in credit card debt and financial hardship.

Retirement Planning: Making too cautious financial decisions might result from retirement anxiety and the concern of outliving one's funds. As a result, returns may be reduced, and retirement savings may be insufficient.

Techniques for Making Emotionally Sensible Financial Decisions

Financial decisions that are made with emotional intelligence must be aware of the effects of emotions and employ good coping mechanisms.

Self-awareness: Begin by becoming aware of your financial and emotional triggers. Recognize when you're feeling afraid, greedy, or nervous, and take a moment to think before acting.

Set Specific Financial Goals: Setting specific financial goals will assist you in making choices that are in line with your long-term aims. Knowing your reasons for investing or saving may be a compass in the middle of emotional turmoil.

Create a Financial Plan: Lay out your income, spending, savings, and assets in a well-structured financial plan. Making decisions that are in line with your financial objectives is easier when you have a strategy to follow.

Consult experts: Look for specialists who can offer unbiased counsel, such as financial advisors. Amid emotional stress, their experience can assist you in making logical judgments.

Avoid Emotional Trading: Emotional trading can result in losses in the realm of investments. Consider using a buy-and-hold investment approach, in which you make long-term investments rather than trading often based on transient emotions.

Develop your patience: Patience is an important characteristic in finance. Recognize that accumulating money takes time, so resist the urge to chase after fast profits or make reckless purchases.

The Right Mix of Reason and Feeling

Emotions have a significant role in decision-making in the world of finance. However, attaining financial success necessitates striking a careful balance between reason and feeling. Although emotions may be a source of inspiration and energy, they must be balanced with reason and self-awareness.

People may make decisions that are in line with their long-term goals by acknowledging the emotional rollercoaster of finances. Individuals may negotiate the ups and downs of this rollercoaster ride with better clarity and resilience by being aware of the emotional triggers that affect financial decisions, ultimately leading to greater financial stability and peace of mind.

Emily's Story: A Journey Through the Financial and Emotional Landscape

A woman called Emily lived in a little village set amid rolling hills. Emily was known for her wit and determination, but when it came to money, she was about to go on a voyage of self-discovery—a trip that would demonstrate the tremendous effect of emotions on financial decisions.

The Pursuit of Wealth

Emily's motivation has always been a desire for financial security. She worked hard in school, got a good career, and started saving carefully. Her journey began on a high note, fueled by ambition and financial ambitions.

The Allure of Greed

Emily got increasingly interested in the world of investing as her funds rose. Her head was flooded with stories of people hitting it rich in the stock market. She was lured by the promise of rapid earnings and the potential of geometrically doubling her money. Greed whispered in her ear, telling her she could beat the odds.

Emily made the foolish decision to invest a major chunk of her resources in a speculative investment that promised huge profits one fateful day. Greed's persuasive voice drove Emily's choice, and she rushed headfirst into the perilous business.

The Depths of Fear

The stock market took an unexpected turn soon after her investment. Prices fell, and Emily watched in terror as her funds vanished in front of her eyes. Fear clutched her heart, and the crushing thought that she would lose everything froze her.

Emily was terrified of financial collapse, and in her despair, she made rash judgments. She liquidated her investments at a loss because she couldn't endure the mental pain of seeing her portfolio fall.

The Agony of Regret

Regret set in as a result of her hasty judgments. Emily bemoaned her rash decisions made in the grip of terror. She recognized that her greedy investment and subsequent panic selling had cost her a lot of money.

Emily's financial decisions were plagued with regret, which became a frequent companion. Even when provided with smart investing options, she questioned her capacity to make solid decisions and resisted re-entering the market.

Finding Balance and Wisdom

Emily's trip through the emotional terrain of finance had been turbulent, but it had also taught her important things. She grasped the need to strike a balance between her financial goals and her emotions.

She sought the advice of an experienced financial counselor, who assisted her in developing a well-structured financial strategy. They worked together to set clear goals, diversify her investments, and underline the significance of having a long-term view.

Emily gradually learned to use her emotions for inspiration while keeping them in check while making financial decisions. She took a patient approach to investing, recognizing that building money was a slow process that required discipline and endurance.

The Triumph of Resilience

Emily's financial status gradually improved over time. Her diverse portfolio expanded, and she attained a degree of financial stability that gave her peace of mind. Her early financial journey's emotional rollercoaster had turned into a steady rise toward her goals.

Emily's story serves as a reminder that emotions may have a significant impact on financial decisions. The route from greed to fear to regret is one that many people have traveled, but it can be handled with knowledge and resilience.

Conclusion: A Harmonious Journey

Emily's story is a timeless allegory about the interaction between emotions and money. It emphasizes the significance of understanding the emotional triggers that drive our financial decisions while striving for a balanced balance of ambition and logic.

Emily's lessons—setting clear goals, diversifying investments, and having a long-term perspective—show that resilience triumphs over emotional distress. Finding this balance allows people to navigate the financial world with greater clarity and confidence, eventually attaining their goals and safeguarding their financial destiny.

Chapter 8

Financial Freedom - The True Meaning of Financial Independence

Many individuals want to achieve financial independence, which is also known as financial freedom. It's a notion that transcends material prosperity or the amassing of possessions. The genuine definition of financial independence includes a wide range of ideas, options, and chances that enable people to live their lives according to their terms.

Financial Independence Definition
Financial independence is essentially the status of having enough money to maintain one's preferred way of life without depending on a regular job or other sources of income. It entails having control over your financial situation and the flexibility to make choices based on your preferences rather than your ability to pay.

Financial independence is about establishing a sense of stability and autonomy in your financial life, not only about owning a specific quantity of money or assets. It's the sensation of knowing you have the means to live comfortably, follow your passions, and deal calmly and stress-free with unforeseen financial difficulties.

The Components of Financial Independence, Deconstructed

Freedom from Financial Stress: Financial independence has as one of its key components freedom from concern and stress related to money. It entails not continuously worrying about money and being able to afford your fundamental requirements, such as shelter, food, healthcare, and education. Getting rid of financial stress is a big step toward financial independence since it may hurt your physical and mental health.

Choice and Autonomy: Financial independence gives you the freedom to make choices. It frees you from the constraints of money so that you can make decisions based on your beliefs and priorities. Financial independence gives you the freedom to choose your life, whether that means pursuing a profession you're passionate about, taking trips across the world, or spending more time with your family. It entails being able to freely say "yes" to possibilities that correspond with your objectives and beliefs and "no" to ones that don't.

Flexible Work Options: Achieving true financial freedom doesn't always require giving up your job. Instead of picking a job only for financial gain, it can mean choosing one that fits your interests and ambitions. This can entail engaging in side jobs, entrepreneurial endeavors, or a rewarding pastime that earns money. You may work on your terms if you have financial freedom, whether it means pursuing a passion project or retiring gradually without feeling under pressure to make ends meet.

Investing in Your Future: The key to achieving financial freedom is investing in your future. It entails having the means to put money toward your long-term objectives, such as retirement savings, supporting your family's financial needs, or contributing to worthy causes. It's the capacity to confidently prepare for the future, knowing that you have the resources to realize your goals. Having financial security enables you to leave a lasting impression on the world and the people you care about.

Peace of Mind: Financial freedom promotes mental tranquility. It entails putting a safety net in place financially to handle unforeseen circumstances, such as medical emergencies or economic downturns, without causing your life's goals to fall apart. It gives you the confidence that you can manage anything life throws at you since you're financially ready for both the anticipated and the unanticipated. You may rest easy at night knowing that you've taken care of your financial security, thanks to this peace of mind.

How to Become Financially Independent

It takes careful preparation, self-control, and patience to reach financial freedom. Building financial stability and independence is a long process, rather than something that happens instantly. These are the major steps on the way:

Define your definition of financial independence while setting goals: What are your goals and financial objectives? Having a distinct understanding of your goals is crucial. Your objectives will direct your financial choices and drive you along the road, whether they be early retirement, global travel, or starting your own business.

Budgeting and saving: Prudent money management is the first step in achieving financial independence. Make a budget that enables you to regularly save money, live within your means, and stay out of debt. You can track your spending, find areas where you can make savings, and commit more money to your financial objectives by using a budget.

Investing wisely: Put your money to work for you by purchasing items with the potential to increase in value over time. To reduce risk and accomplish your long-term financial goals, diversify your investments. Investing is a crucial part of accumulating money and may swiftly advance your path to financial freedom.

Continuous Learning: Financial markets and economic situations are constantly changing. Making educated judgments may be aided by maintaining knowledge of personal finances, investments, and economic trends. Your ability to manage the complexity of the financial world with skill and confidence is enhanced by financial literacy.

Living Within Your Means: Living within your means is one of the keys to financial freedom. Avoid falling into the lifestyle inflation trap when rising income causes rising expenditure. Place more emphasis on investing and conserving the difference. Being frugal can help you accumulate wealth and hasten your path to financial freedom.

Building Multiple Income Streams: Consider diversifying your revenue streams while creating many streams of income. Your ability to prosper financially may be hampered if you just work regular jobs. Investigate ways to earn extra money, such as launching a side company, making real estate investments, or creating passive income streams. Having several sources of income increases your financial stability and flexibility.

Seeking Professional Advice: As your financial position grows more complex, financial advisers and specialists can offer insightful advice. They can assist you in developing a financial strategy based on your objectives and risk tolerance. Making wise judgments may be easier with the support of a reliable adviser who can offer unbiased advice.

Beyond Cents and Dollars: A Meaningful Life

The ability to live a life that is in line with your beliefs, passions, and objectives is what makes financial independence beautiful. It enables you to concentrate on the things that are most important to you, such as spending more time with your loved ones, seeking out enriching experiences, or having a constructive influence on the world.

Financial freedom is a journey that may be both gratifying and transforming, rather than a final destination. It's about obtaining a level of financial security that improves your quality of life overall and gives you the tools to live a fulfilling life. The freedom and opportunities that money may provide are more important than just the money itself.

Imagine having the financial stability to live life on your terms and waking up each morning knowing that you can follow your goals. Imagine the calmness that comes from knowing you are ready for whatever problems or possibilities may arise. A life enhanced by freedom, options, and the pursuit of what makes you happy and fulfilled is what financial independence truly means.

As you set out on your path to financial independence, keep in mind that the goal isn't only to acquire a certain level of wealth; it's also to feel the immense sense of empowerment and pleasure that comes with it. In the end, having a life well lived is about designing a life that matches your beliefs and objectives.

Sarah's Journey: Understanding the Real Meaning of Financial Independence

There was a woman named Sarah who resided in a busy metropolis. She had always worked hard and diligently, but her financial situation was a continuous cause of worry. Sarah would have significant revelations and life-changing transformations as a result of her quest to understand the actual meaning of financial freedom.

The Daily Grind

Sarah felt stuck in the never-ending cycle of bills and costs despite having reliable work, a good income, and a nice apartment. Her monthly income appeared to vanish in a flurry of rent, electricity, food, and loan repayments. She experienced the impression of being a hamster on a wheel, running continuously but never getting anywhere because of her financial responsibilities.

Defining Financial Independence

One day, Sarah overheard a discussion on financial independence while enjoying a cup of coffee at a nearby café. She became intrigued by the idea and started doing some investigation. Sarah came to realize that gaining financial independence meant more than just having a sizable bank account; it meant feeling secure, free, and autonomous in one's financial life.

Goal-setting

With greater clarity on her financial goals, Sarah established specific objectives for herself. She wished for freedom from the ongoing stress of living paycheck to paycheck and the freedom to follow her hobbies. Sarah pictured a life in which choosing to work was an option rather than a necessity.

Budgeting and Savings

To begin with, Sarah made a budget that would allow her to live within her means. She reduced wasteful expenditures, prepared meals at home, and meticulously monitored her spending. Sarah saw an increase in her sense of financial control as she increased her savings and decreased her debt.

Investing in Knowledge

Sarah engaged herself in books, podcasts, and seminars about personal finance and investment after realizing the value of financial literacy. She gained knowledge about the effectiveness of compounding, the advantages of diversity, and the value of a long-term viewpoint.

Building Multiple Income Streams

Sarah looked for ways to get money on the side. She began a side business selling her handmade jewelry, which not only generated extra income but also gave her the freedom to follow her passion for creativity. These extra sources of income gave her a safety net and sped up her progress toward financial security.

Consulting a Professional

As Sarah's financial position grew more complicated, she looked for financial adviser advice. The consultant assisted her in developing a thorough financial strategy customized to her objectives. They looked over her investments, changed her asset allocation, and made sure her financial choices were in line with her long-term goals.

Embracing Financial Independence

After some time, Sarah's life changed. She had eliminated her debt, gathered a sizable emergency fund, and created a diverse investment portfolio. A sense of stability and calm had taken the place of the burden of financial worry.

To make ends meet, Sarah no longer felt forced to work at a job she disliked. Instead, even though it paid less, she picked a job that was in line with her passions. She was free to travel, spend time with family, and pursue new interests. Sarah was living life on her own and had achieved financial freedom.

What Financial Independence Means

Through her path, Sarah came to understand that gaining financial independence was about living a full and purposeful life, not simply about riches or money. It meant having the freedom and resources to follow one's passions, to make decisions that are consistent with one's principles, and to have peace of mind.

Sarah was able to concentrate on what was important to her—the delight of creation, the coziness of interpersonal relationships, and the beauty of taking in the marvels of life—thanks to her financial freedom. Her voyage had not only improved her financial situation but also deepened her spirit.

A Life Well Lived, in Summary

Sarah's experience serves as a reminder that achieving financial independence is not just a lofty ideal but also an attainable reality. Setting clear goals, living within your means, investing in education, and obtaining expert advice when necessary are the first steps on this path. It is a path that enables people to shatter the bonds of financial stress and welcome a life full of meaning, freedom, and joy.

Sarah concluded that the true meaning of financial freedom was not found in the figures on a bank account but rather in the smiles, laughter, and meaningful moments that filled her life as she sat in her little café and observed the outside world. She had traveled a path that had brought her to a position of genuine richness and a life well lived.

Chapter 9

Lessons from Historical Financial Events - Illuminating the Path to Financial Wisdom

We may learn a great deal from past financial catastrophes, which range from the Great Depression of the 1930s through the Dot-Com Bubble of the early 2000s and the Global Financial Crisis of 2008. These occasions have had a significant impact on economies, financial systems, and personal lives. We may learn valuable lessons from them that direct us toward financial knowledge and resilience by studying them.

Diversification is important

A sobering cautionary tale about the dangers of placing all of your financial eggs in one basket is the Great Depression of the 1930s. Due to their excessive concentration on a small number of equities, many investors during that period experienced significant losses.

Lesson: To lower risk, diversify your assets across different asset classes and businesses. Market volatility can be more successfully weathered by a well-balanced portfolio.

The Dangers of Speculative Mania 2

The late 1990s and early 2000s Dot-Com Bubble were characterized by excessive optimism and skyrocketing stock prices for internet-related businesses. However, many investors saw their portfolios tank as the bubble broke.

Lesson: Steer clear of "get-rich-quick" scams and speculative bubbles. When purchasing assets that look too wonderful to be true, use caution.

Risk management is important

The 2008 global financial crisis revealed the financial system's weaknesses. It served as a wake-up call on the risks of taking excessive risks, especially in the property market, which had far-reaching effects.

Lesson: Evaluate and control your financial risks. Avoid taking on excessive debt, and make sure your assets are in line with your level of risk tolerance.

The Benefit of a Long-Term View

Financial developments throughout history serve as a reminder of the advantages of long-term investing. Markets may endure brief volatility, but they usually bounce back and expand over time.

Lesson: Maintain your long-term investing plan despite market declines. Steer clear of forming snap judgments based on momentary swings.

The Impossibility of Predicting Black Swan Events

Rare and unforeseeable catastrophes known as "black swan events," such as the 9/11 terrorist attacks or the COVID-19 pandemic, can have a significant effect on the financial markets and the global economy.

Lesson: Recognize the inherent unpredictability of black swan events. Create a solid financial strategy with an emergency reserve to handle unforeseen situations.

The Need for Financial Education

The significance of financial literacy is underscored by historical occurrences. Due to their ignorance of complicated financial goods and institutions, many people were unprepared for financial disasters.

Lesson: Spend money on developing your financial literacy. To make wise judgments, you need to have a fundamental understanding of personal finance, investments, and economic principles.

The Function of Regulatory Control

Increased regulatory monitoring to avert future crises is frequently the result of financial crises. The objectives of these rules are to safeguard customers and keep financial systems stable.

Lesson: Keep up with financial laws and how they could affect your financial choices. Your financial security depends on your ability to comply with the rules.

The Strength of Resilience

Even the most disastrous financial crises may be overcome by people and economies. This resiliency is evidence of human adaptability and recovery power.

Lesson: Create financial resilience by keeping a diverse investment portfolio, paying down debt, and setting up an emergency fund.

The Benefits of a Balanced Approach

Individuals may weather financial storms and accomplish long-term goals by adopting a balanced approach to money that includes saving, investing, and smart spending.

Lesson: Make a well-balanced financial plan that takes into consideration both your immediate needs and long-term goals. Aim towards a financially viable way of living.

The Lifelong Learning Journey

Financial events in history serve as a reminder of how crucial it is to stay educated and adjust to shifting economic conditions. Financial well-being depends on continuous learning since financial systems change.

Lesson: Commit to continuing your education in personal finance and investing. Observe developments in the financial markets and trends in the economy.

Financial history reveals trends, tendencies, and weaknesses that continue to influence our financial system. We may traverse the financial world of today with more knowledge, resiliency, and the capacity to make decisions that are advantageous to our financial well-being by studying these events and the lessons they provide.

The John Templeton Lesson: Getting Through Financial Crisis Depths

Legendary investor and philanthropist John Templeton left behind a body of financial knowledge that was forged in the fire of significant financial events. The lessons we may learn from these occurrences are attested to by his life narrative.

John Templeton set off on an amazing voyage at the beginning of the 1930s, at the height of the Great Depression. He made the audacious decision to invest $10,000 (approximately $200,000 now), fresh out of Yale University, in the stock market, despite the time's economic unrest. But he did it in the thick of the New York City crisis, not in the United States. His justification was straightforward but profound: "People are afraid. When prices are low, I can purchase more shares for my money.

Lesson 1: Thinking in Opposition

We may learn from Templeton's contrarian stance during the Great Depression about the importance of having alternative perspectives while facing a financial crisis. Instead of giving in to anxiety and worry, he saw a chance to purchase assets at a bargain. His financial theory became known for its contrarian outlook.

Templeton's wager was quite profitable. As the economy started to recover over the following several years, the value of his assets increased dramatically. He had greatly increased his capital while simultaneously protecting it.

Lesson 2: A Long-Term View

Templeton kept displaying a long-term outlook as his profession developed. His trades ranged throughout the world, from Japanese equities to European bonds. His strategy was not dictated by passing market trends but rather by a conviction in the possibility of long-term value and growth.

Lesson 3: Risk Management and Diversification

By diversifying his assets across many asset classes and geographical areas, Templeton was able to shield his portfolio from the volatility of certain markets. He recognized the value of risk management and refrained from investing all of his resources in one single area.

Lesson 4: The Influence of Research and Discipline

Templeton was renowned for his meticulous study throughout his life and for maintaining his composure in the face of market volatility. He believed in doing in-depth analyses of potential investment possibilities, searching for cheap assets, and maintaining the discipline to stick to his investing approach.

Lesson 5: Being Generous

As his wealth increased, Templeton committed himself to philanthropy. He gave out a large percentage of his income to causes that supported science, religion, and education. His dedication to charitable giving serves as evidence that real riches comprise more than just material possessions; they also include the influence we may have on the world.

The astonishing experiences of John Templeton during the Great Depression and his subsequent financial accomplishments serve as an example of the lessons that may be learned from past financial occurrences. His unconventional thinking, long-term outlook, diversification, self-discipline, and dedication to giving back provide insightful guidance for navigating the financial world's difficulties.

The wisdom of historical events is eternal

The biography of John Templeton serves as a reminder that even the most traumatic financial disasters in history may yield invaluable lessons. They show us that, for those who face crises with a clear and logical perspective, opportunities may occur. In managing our funds, they place a strong emphasis on the necessity of discipline, inquiry, diversification, and long-term planning.

Even if we are unable to forecast when the next financial crisis will arise, we can learn from past mistakes to help us make wise choices and develop our financial resilience. In our ongoing quest for financial security, the timeless wisdom of historical events—as expressed by people like John Templeton—serves as a beacon of illumination.

Conclusion

Money and Happiness - Wrapping up the lessons

Our exploration of the complex relationship between wealth and contentment reveals a wealth of insightful truths that may help us lead lives that are more balanced and rewarding. Our comprehension of the complex tango between these two realities is something we explore throughout our lives.

Lesson 1: Wealth is not everything

We've come to understand that, even though money is necessary for meeting our fundamental necessities and maintaining our comfort, real happiness goes well beyond monetary success. It exists in the ethereal worlds of interpersonal relationships, purpose, and personal development. Although it can provide people with the means to pursue these deeper types of happiness, money itself is not the goal.

Lesson 2: Striking a Balance

Finding happiness requires striking a fine balance. Pursuing our hobbies and working toward financial stability does not have to conflict. We've found that balancing money and happiness may be achieved by matching our financial decisions with our beliefs and objectives. Our ability to live with meaning and joy may be facilitated by a carefully thought-out financial path.

Lesson 3: The Influence of Mentality

Our mental attitude is crucial to both our material and emotional well-being. We have seen how developing appreciation, engaging in financial awareness, and embracing a growth mindset may alter our perception of money and increase happiness.

Lesson 4: The Influence of Giving

Giving has become recognized as one of the most effective pathways to pleasure. Sharing our resources, whether they be financial or personal, benefits us as well as others around us. Money and happiness go hand in hand, as evidenced by the satisfaction of changing the world for the better.

Lesson 5: Looking for Meaning in Your Purpose

We've spoken about how important it is to have a purpose in all we do, whether it be through fulfilling jobs, artistic endeavors, or community service. Although money may be used as a tool to assist these initiatives, the alignment with our mission ultimately results in genuine fulfillment.

Lesson 6: The Financial Resilience Wisdom

Happiness is built on the foundation of financial resilience. To establish a solid financial foundation, we now understand the importance of setting aside money for savings, investing properly, and handling debt responsibly. We can confidently handle life's uncertainties thanks to our resilience.

Lesson 7: The Beauty of Financial Independence

We've learned that financial independence is about freedom and choice as much as it is about money. It gives us the freedom to live life on our terms, follow our passions, and make choices that are consistent with our beliefs. It's a trip that enables us to get over the restrictions of our financial means.

Lesson 8: The Light of Learning

Our research has shown that the key to balancing wealth and happiness is to constantly learn new things. Being knowledgeable about investments, personal money, and economic trends enables us to make wise decisions and adjust to changing situations.

These teachings act as our compass in the complex world of wealth and pleasure. They serve as a reminder that while money may be a tool for improving our well-being, its ultimate value is found in how well it aligns with our more fundamental objectives and aspirations. May we keep these lessons in mind as we negotiate the complex relationship between wealth and happiness, enabling them to show us the way to a life that is richer in joy and meaning?